My Choice or God's Choice

My Choice or God's Choice

When Waiting on God Leads to Marital Bliss

WANDALA MORRIS

COOKE HOUSE
PUBLISHING

Winston-Salem, NC

My Choice or God's Choice: When Waiting On God Leads to Marital Bliss
Copyright © 2025 by Wandala Morris

All rights reserved. No part of this publication may be reproduced or transmitted in any form or by any means electronic or mechanical, including photocopy, recording, or any information storage and retrieval system now known or to invented, without permission in writing from the author, except by a reviewer who wish to quote brief passages in connection with a review written for inclusion in a magazine, newspaper, website, or broadcast.

Unless otherwise identified, Scripture quotations are from the King James Version. Copyright © 1982 by Thomas Nelson, Inc. Used by permission. All rights reserved.

ISBN: 979-8-3485-3277-2

Cooke House Publishing
(a division of Cooke Classic Branding & Design, LLC)
www.cookeclassic.com/chp
publishing@cookeclassic.com

Published in the United States of America. First Edition

Acknowledgments

I first give all praise and honor to my Lord and Savior Jesus Christ for His everlasting mercy. Even when I did wrong, He kept me.

I give honor to my husband, Mr. Terry Morris, a man after God's own heart and mine. He was the love of my life.

To my mom, Annette Balkcom, who was a true woman of God who loved and instilled love in all her children.

To my brothers Thomas, Darryl, and Edward.

To my Aunt Pat, my safe place. The one who constantly loved and prayed with me. The one I ran to for comfort and support. The one who opened up her heart and home to me.

To my friend, Minister Kathy Fullenwider, for sharing her time, input, and prayers with me.

To Reverend Margie Clark, who was definitely godsent to get me through so many crises.

Thank you to all who prayed for me, encouraged me, listened to me, spent time with me, opened your doors to me, never judged me, but understood that we all go through and don't always get it right. But thank God for His grace and mercy. It never fails.

I love and thank you all for allowing the Lord to use you to be a blessing to me.

Contents

Preface	9
Chapter 1 The Man I Chose	14
Chapter 2 The Wedding Day	19
Chapter 3 Married Life	22
Chapter 4 The Repentance Stage	25
Chapter 5 Breakthrough Stage	26
Chapter 6 Divorce	27
Chapter 7 Enticed Back and Delivered Again	29
Chapter 8 Thanking God for Deliverance	31
Chapter 9 God's Choice for Me	33
Chapter 10 Life and Financial Planning Begins	38
Chapter 11 Our Churches	41
Chapter 12 Second Wedding Preparations Begin	43
Chapter 13 Our Marriage Agreement	46
Chapter 14 Our New Home	48
Chapter 15 Ministering in Song Together	49
Chapter 16 Traumatic Ending to My Perfect Marriage	51
Chapter 17 Dream of Victory	54
Chapter 18 Restored	56
Chapter 19 Conclusion	58
About the Author	59

Preface

Life is about choices. We can choose to make the right decisions, or we can choose to make the wrong ones. If we allow our emotions to make decisions that are not pleasing unto God, there will be consequences. But know that if we call on Him and ask for His forgiveness and direction, He is there to forgive, lighten the load, and direct us.

There are many reasons we make poor decisions in life. Some of those are fear, loneliness, impatience, lack, lust, love, or simply not applying God's Word to our lives. Growing up, I would hear people say that you reap what you sow, be it good or bad. I know that to be true, as many of you do as well. Therefore, we must think before we act because the consequences of our decisions could last a lifetime. Often, we enter into relationships not ordained by God, which leads to physical, mental, and emotional pain not only for ourselves but towards the people we love. Innocent children are brought into this world into hostile, unsafe environments. We lose precious time in life we can never get back. We not only lose family and friends, but opportunities and gifts that God wanted for us.

Although Christ has His plan for us, He gives us the freedom and ability to make choices. In Joshua 24:15, God gave Israel a choice to decide whom they would serve, whether they chose the Lord or the gods of the Amorites or gods of their fathers. Joshua and his household chose to serve the Lord. The Bible tells us in James 1:22 to be doers of the Word and not hearers only, but it's very important that we listen. To be in the will of God, which limits our mistakes and unhappiness, we must learn to listen for God to speak before we take action. John 10:4-5 tells us that sheep hear their shepherd's voice and a stranger they will not follow because the stranger's voice is unknown. Ask God to clear your mind of the daily stress and anxiety of this world, so you will hear Him with clarity when He speaks.

While we are here on earth, Christ wants us to serve Him with gladness, expressing His love daily to others. It's very important that we spend time with God to know Him and His ways and what His plan is for our future. We do this by studying His Word and increasing our prayer life. There are several methods God may use to reveal His plan to us; it may be through scripture, dreams, visions, and sometimes, through others.

Once we realize that serving God and expressing His love to others is both a blessing and an honor, doors of opportunity will open. The Lord will place us in the presence of those that will be a blessing to us. Ideas will flow, leading to career and financial success. Being a pastor, evangelist, deacon, missionary, musician, Sunday morning only Christian, or everyday Christian doesn't prevent one from sinning or making wrong decisions. We all sin and come short of the glory of God. But through confession and repentance, we have access to a Father who is waiting to forgive us. And if we confess our faults and ask for forgiveness, the Bible tells us we will be forgiven!

If you are in a place right now in your life where you need to make a decision, trust God!

Scripture to live by: Trust in the Lord with all thine heart; and lean not unto thine own understanding. In all thy ways acknowledge him, and he shall direct thy paths. (Proverbs 3:5-6)

Important Decisions

Besides choosing Christ as your personal savior, choosing the person to share the rest of your life with is one of the most important decisions you'll face. Growing up, we all have dreams and fantasies about the characteristics of the person we want to marry. We imagine what they may look like, including their hair, perfect teeth, and smooth skin. We imagine their successful career, income status, where they're from, where we'll live, how many children we'll have, and of course, you imagine being head over hills in love. There is an old saying that beauty is in the eyes of the beholder. I believe that saying. God created all of us differently, yet the same being in His image. There is nothing wrong with relaying to God the characteristics of the spouse you desire. Philippians 4:6 says, "Be careful for nothing; but in every thing by prayer and supplication with thanksgiving let your requests be made known unto God."

Please listen to God and He will answer you. Jeremiah 33:3 declares, "Call unto me, and I will answer thee, and show thee great and mighty things, which thou knowest not." According to society, some people are considered beautiful or attractive based on their physicality, while others may be considered less attractive based on the outer appearance. However, being attractive is not just about the outside appearance, but also about one's character. Are they faithful, truthful, loving, sincere, comforting, encouraging, and intelligent? Do they walk upright before God and man? Or when you really look at the person, do you see someone who is mean, envious, selfish, unloving, controlling, lacking kindness, self-indulgent, or possesses a spirit of deceit?

The way a person genuinely cares about you, themselves, and others tells so much about them. Although you may marry someone that does not fit society's standard of beauty, that does not hinder you from experiencing true love from that person, nor does marrying someone that is physically attractive guarantee marital happiness.

Christ knows your heart and knows the characteristics of the person who you're attracted to. More importantly, He knows what's best for you. There is nothing wrong with having your preferences, but always ask Christ to make the final decision. When it comes to my choice or God's choice, I'll choose His every time!

Christ wants us to be loved. He wants us to have that special someone to share life with. He enjoys seeing us happy and fulfilled. Christ wants to give us the desires of our heart according to His will, but we must:

Pray. Ask God for what you want. Matthew 7:7 says, "Ask, and it shall be given you; seek, and ye shall find; knock, and it shall be opened unto you."

Be Obedient. Obey the answer from God. Galatians 5:17 says, "For the flesh lusteth against the Spirit, and the Spirit against the flesh and these are contrary the one to the other, so that ye cannot do the things that ye would." Psalm 143:10 states, "Teach me to do thy will; for thy art my God: thy spirit is good; lead me to the land of uprightness."

As you read my testimony, I pray that:

You are inspired to wait on God and not allow yourself to commit to any relationship out of haste. You wait to hear God speak.

You listen to the counsel of your elders, who God has placed to instruct you through the Word.

You watch for signs that God is not pleased with your decisions. You love yourself enough to realize your value, not accepting less than what God has for you.

You are proud of who you are and the family in which you were born.

You hold on to who you are, while joining together as a couple.

You see the heart of the person before committing.

You come to repentance by the Holy Spirit.

Regardless of the mistakes you make, you realize God has your back! He loves you so much. He said He will never leave you nor forsake you. Please remember, when our plan fails and the choices we make crumble, God's plan will stand.

Although this book is short, it has taken me six years to complete. Hurt, sadness, loneliness, and anxiety can take a major toll on you. It makes it difficult to function in everyday life. Things that were once so simple became extremely difficult, like working, daily chores, and personal care.

I was twenty-seven years old and living at home. I was saved, single, never married, no boyfriend, and no children when my stepfather who raised me died. That was the first time I realized that life wasn't forever. After a while, my brothers no longer lived in the family home. It was just my mom and me. I was always sensitive to my mom's feelings, so I could see the sadness and struggle that she was going through because of my stepfather's death. I, too, was in an emotional struggle. During this time, my mother and I grew even closer. We had a mother-daughter relationship, and we were also best friends.

The Man I Chose

Three years after my stepfather passed away, the house next door to my mom's became vacant, and soon after, a young man moved in. My mother was her normal self, friendly to our new neighbor as she talked to him across our chain-link fence. She introduced herself and me as her daughter. I wasn't attracted to his outward appearance, but there was something about the way he projected himself that attracted me. He was of medium build and height and carried himself in a mature manner. He spoke with a smooth, enticing voice. He seemed to be a hard worker. I saw no visitors at his home. He had a dog in his yard that he didn't seem to pay much attention to. He drove an old hatchback work truck, and I learned he worked in construction.

From what I could see, he was a man of routine. He was quiet, respectable, and kept to himself. He would leave his house about 7:00 am and return home around 3:30 pm daily. Once he was home, he never changed out of his work clothes, so he was always dirty and sweaty. After arriving home from work, he would immediately begin working in his yard or on the inside of the house.

As time went by, he and I would make small talk over the fence. One day, while casually talking, I asked him if he would like to go to the local fair that was in town, and he said yes. I remember it was a Saturday evening, and this was the first time in the month or so that he lived there that he was not in work attire. He was showered, neat, and casually dressed. Although he was clean and neat, he was not a trendy dresser. It was obvious he didn't have a lot of money, a sense of fashion, nor invested in his attire. Although I was not physically attracted to him, I found his respectable and polite manner attractive. I loved how he spoke softly with a sexy northern accent and with a smile that was oh so captivating. Little did I know that was the beginning of a nightmare for me.

As we continued communicating, he opened up to me regarding the status of the home he was now living in. He told me he was renting the house. Down the road, if the owner of the property decided, he would then rent-to-own the house. His credit was not good, and he didn't have money for a down payment on a new property. The house was an older home, and because he was a construction worker, he could work on remodeling it himself.

I spent time with him at his home, with most of our conversations being about his dreams of owning the home he was renting. We never went out on any dates other than the fair. I was definitely not accustomed to this. My past relationships always included dinner, movie dates, events, performances, trips, cruises, parties, flowers, gifts, laughing, having fun, and hanging out with friends and family. None of those things happened with this relationship. The death of my stepfather put me in an unfamiliar state of mind about life, which caused me to settle for less than what God had for me. It made me realize that life wasn't forever and could end at any moment. Therefore, I made rash decisions that I would not have normally made.

I honestly don't recall the details of him asking me to marry him, but he did. And because I don't remember, it shows how special it wasn't. I remember it was within a few months after we met, but I did not answer him right away. I said I would think about it, and he was okay with that. I told my mom and asked what she thought. My mom said it was my decision, but I could tell she was not thrilled at all. Deep inside, I knew he was not the one for me. I was getting older, and he was the first man to ask me to marry him, so I did not want to miss out on the opportunity. Eventually, I said yes. I told him the type of home and area I would like to live, but he said he wanted us to live in the house he was renting. When I asked why, he stated it would make him feel a part of the plan for our home together. It would be his contribution to what would be our home since he didn't have money to contribute to the purchase and had already done some remodeling on the current property. Since I had lived next door for approximately twenty years since childhood, I was eager to move to another neighborhood to start fresh. But I wanted him to be happy, so I agreed to live there. My mother and I were both working and had a little money saved up. My fiancé said it was the bride and her family who were financially responsible for the wedding. So, my mother being the loving mom, stepped right up to make the day special for me. Between the two of us, we took care of all the wedding details.

  My fiancé told his landlord that he was getting married and wanted to start the rent-to-own process, but the landlord said he wanted to sell it. Because my fiancé did not have good credit or money for the down payment, he asked me to put up the down payment and put the house in my name and then add his name to the deed afterwards. I was hesitant but agreed. In the process of buying the house, we were also searching for a church and minister to perform the wedding ceremony. What a challenge that was!

  When my stepfather, who was the pastor of the church I attended, passed away, another minister in the church stepped up as the acting pastor. I told him I was getting married and asked if he would perform the ceremony. He said yes. Later that evening, he called and asked me who was I marrying. When I told him, he said, "I'm sorry. I can't perform the ceremony because that man is not saved." I knew he was not saved. I also know the Word of God says we are not to be unequally yoked with unbelievers, but I took it lightly and was disobedient. This was the choice I made. Being turned down by a minister to perform my wedding was a little embarrassing, but I continued on.

  I then talked to a friend whose pastor was a woman whom I knew as well. My friend suggested I ask her to perform the ceremony. I thought that was a good idea. I called and spoke with the pastor, and she made an appointment to meet with both of us in her church office. When we arrived, she greeted me as always with a warm smile and asked us to have a seat. As soon as we both sat down, she looked at me, looked at him, turned to me again and said, "You can do better than this! This man is not saved! I can't perform this wedding." She kept repeating, "You can do better than this!" I could see the anger on his face, but he did not say one word to this powerful woman of God. Again, I was embarrassed, so I said thank you and we left.

I was getting disappointed. I knew he was not saved, but he was nice and I liked him. To this day, I never recall telling him I loved him or him saying he loved me. I told him that being a Christian, I was not supposed to marry someone unless they were saved too. I think he could see I was a little sad now. I really cannot explain why I agreed to marry him, other than that it was a plan of deception from Satan himself. The enemy knew God had His plan of prosperity for me, and he knew God had a work for me to do. Satan knew I loved the Lord and had a willing heart to serve Him. He also knew my weakness, which was a fear of getting older and being alone. My fears opened the door for Satan to interrupt God's plan for my life.

Someone told me about another pastor who had a huge church and officiated weddings for a small fee. I called the church, spoke with the secretary, paid the one-hundred-dollar fee, and she reserved the date for the wedding. All we had to do was show up and the church would provide the pastor, musicians, and singers. When I told my fiancé, we were both excited. Since I was not familiar with this church or the pastor, we attended the following Sunday service. The church was beautiful. The other two churches were much smaller, one was a storefront church. We sat through the service, which was not what I was accustomed to. I grew up in a Pentecostal church where the members spoke in tongues, were being filled with the spirit, and there was the laying on of hands. The services were lively where everyone was like family and treated visitors like family as well.

This church was like the old time Baptist church. They sang hymns, and the prayers seemed memorized. The atmosphere was not joyful, nor were the members friendly. It really did not feel like the presence of God was there, although I know He is everywhere. At the end of the message, the pastor asked if anyone wanted to give their life to Christ to come to the altar. I was shocked when my fiancé got up and walked down the long aisle to the front of the church, along with several other people, to give his life to Christ. The pastor said a prayer asking God to save them and to change their lives. I have to say that I was truly disappointed the pastor didn't lead them in the sinner's prayer or give them any information about salvation. I can only speak for myself. If I were not saved and did not know Jesus as my Lord and Savior, I don't believe I would know any more about giving my life to Christ as I did before I walked to the altar. After service, I told my fiancé that I was surprised to see him go to the altar, and he said, "Well, you said you wanted to be married to someone who was saved." I know God is the one that changes hearts and minds, so I did not judge his sincerity when he said he was now saved; that was between him and God. But I believed he went to the altar to comfort me in my choice to be his wife.

Now that we had a venue set, it was time to make the other plans. I talked to my fiancé about things we needed to do next to prepare for the wedding. He told me it was the bride and her family that were supposed to take care of all the wedding plans and financial responsibilities that go along with it. As the groom, his responsibility was the honeymoon. Again, I agreed. My mother and I started preparing for the big day. She happily did what she could to make this day special for me. Between us working together, we moved things along.

My fiancé's sister came for the wedding and her young daughter was there to be the flower girl. I remember my fiancé said that his sister bought his niece a dress for the wedding, but she didn't have any shoes. He thought it was right that I bought her shoes. So, I did. My fiancé's father also came to town for the wedding. He appeared to be very poised and quiet. He was not what I expected since my fiancé told me that his father physically abused and battered his mom, who was now deceased. He seemed hurt when he spoke about the physical abuse his mother suffered by his father's hand.

By this time, the closing of the house had taken place. The attorney my fiancé found said once all the paperwork went through and everything was finalized, I could then add his name to the deed. That sounded good to both of us.

The Wedding Day

The wedding was soon after the closing of the house. Interestingly enough, on the day of my wedding, I moved in slow motion. I was not eager as a bride would normally be. I was just going through the motions. I had no strong feelings towards this man. I was not in love with him. I just liked him. I truly believe the Spirit of God within me was grieved.

My mom told me she had decided not to go. Wow! I could see the hurt and sadness on her face. I said, "Ma, you have to come." She attended the wedding, but she knew that this wedding should not happen because God did not ordain it. She knew he was not the man for me. Although this was supposed to be my big day, I was not enthusiastic about it. I really did not see a future in this marriage.

I arrived at the church three hours late because I wasn't in a hurry to get there. It was not intentional; I was just in a calm, unhurried state. I just knew everybody would be gone, but the church was full of people. Most of the guests were my family and my mother's friends, along with my fiancé's father, sister, and niece. Also, a woman I knew he had supposedly stopped seeing was sitting at the very back of the church. The wedding party had all entered the church and was in place.

Now it was time for the ring barrier, which was my four-year-old nephew. (During the rehearsals, everyone in the wedding party did an excellent job, especially my little nephew, who was the apple of my mom's eye.) My nephew walked down the aisle just as we rehearsed looking so handsome, then suddenly, he takes off running between the benches, up and down the aisles, screaming, "No! No! No! No!" His mom and other people ran frantically behind him; it was a bit chaotic for a while. Finally, his mom caught up with him, calmed him down, and retrieved the rings. Any other bride would have been mortified had this happened at her wedding, but it really did not bother me. I was the least bit concerned about how it looked.

As I look back, I realize that incident was my final warning not to marry that man. God gave me one last warning through a child. I did not hear what God was telling me. I understand now that we must not only open our eyes and ears, but our hearts as well, so we will hear and do God's will. God speaks to us in various ways. He spoke to me through two ministers who told me they would not perform the ceremony. He spoke to me through the hurt I saw in my mother. He spoke to me through all the efforts that I put in planning the wedding while my fiancé put in no effort or concern for any financial responsibilities. Christ spoke to me through a child! Last but certainly not least, Christ spoke to my heart because on my wedding day, I really felt no sense of urgency or excitement about getting married.

Despite it all, I felt beautiful as I walked down the aisle, but I was not happy. I wore a gorgeous, long, white fitted beaded gown, with a long train and veil, with white satin shoes. My hair was full of curls. Our wedding was very classy. The bridesmaids wore exquisite, long, straight black evening gowns with a large open white collar. The men wore black tuxedos with white cummerbunds and shirts. The sanctuary was striking; there was also a floral decorated arch that really stood out.

My mother and aunts decorated the house for the wedding reception, and it was elegant. There were flowers, balloons, and a gorgeous table setting with lots of food. Another table had many cards and gifts given by my relatives, friends, and coworkers. There was only one present from anyone that my husband knew. It was a set of candleholders, which I thought was very nice. After a few hours at our reception having a wonderful time, it was time to leave for our honeymoon. My husband had made reservations in Key West, Florida, which is about 154 miles south of Miami. My mother and aunts stayed at the house to clean up. I gave my mom a big hug, and she said to drive carefully.

Off we went. We had great conversation on our way to Key West. Once we were in our hotel room, I made a quick call to my mom and told her we had arrived safely. She said, "Okay, yawl have a good time." I was on the phone for no longer than ten seconds, and as soon as I hung up, the *real* man I married showed up. He was furious I called my mom. I could not believe it; he was angry. I tried to explain to him I simply wanted my mom to know we made it okay. He spent the next few hours telling me I should not have called my mom—that I was his wife, and it was now just the two of us. I was so hurt, and on our honeymoon night, without either of us saying the words, our marriage ended. I was not going to stop communicating with my mom. Of course, there was no lovemaking that night because the love was not there. I didn't even like him at this moment.

Married Life

The original plan was to stay in Key West, Florida, for one week, but because of what happened on the first night, we headed back to Miami the next morning. I was a little afraid to go next door and say hello to my mom, so to keep the peace, I didn't. The hurt from that was so devastatingly sad for me, and I know it was for her as well. During the next few weeks, we tried to function as a newly married couple, but it was not a happy time.

I remember one day I stopped and bought a burger before coming home. Once I arrived home, I began eating the burger. Suddenly, he says to me, "I hope you don't choke." When he said that, there was such a mean, hateful look on his face. I could feel the evil, which made me feel uneasy.

My mother wanted to keep the peace with him as well. One day, she came over to our house and asked him to come outside. She sat in a chair across from him at the table outside with tears rolling down her face. My mom said, "When I leave this earth, I just want to know that my daughter is happy and she has somebody to take care of her." He looked at her with no compassion. Neither of them knew I saw and heard that conversation. My mother was sad about what I was going through; she knew I was not happy. She told me she would sit close to the window in her house, so if needed, she would come to my rescue. My mom was concerned about my safety and happiness. I knew she would sacrifice herself and her own happiness for me.

My husband was a very suspicious man. One day, he came home from work and went into the bathroom. When he came out, he asked why were there two washcloths in the bathroom, neither of which was his. I explained that I always use two washcloths, one for my face and the other for the remainder of my body. I used a separate cleanser on my face because my skin was very sensitive. He obviously did not believe me, insinuating someone else had been there and used a washcloth. On another occasion, my husband raped me. There are some people who believe your husband can not rape you, but I'm a witness that it happens, and it happened to me. This man was full of anger and rage for no apparent reason. He threw me on the bed, forcing himself inside me while forcibly sodomizing me with an object. The physical pain was horrible. I was afraid of him, too afraid to scream. It was painful physically and emotionally. I wanted so much to scream for help, but I was afraid of what he might do to me. I knew that my mother, who was right next door would hear, and I did not want her to come over and he hurt her. I endured it while sobbing.

On another occasion, I found condoms in the pockets of his clothes. We never used condoms, so I knew he was having sexual relations outside of our marriage. Based on a conversation I had with the uncle of his previous girlfriend who was at our wedding, they were still seeing each other.

Our wedding was in early November. I don't recall anything special about our Thanksgiving together. That's how exciting it was, but I remember Christmas. His older brother came into town to visit him, and on Christmas Day, he and his brother left the house and went to the movies, so he said. They were gone all day! So, I spent our first and only Christmas alone.

I was so angry; I picked up the Christmas tree and threw it out the front door, with all the lights and decorations still on it. I watched as neighbors walked by, pointing, whispering, and laughing about the tree. He finally came home as if everything was okay and quietly asked why I threw the tree out the door. I had nothing to say; he knew why. Because he was the kind of man who wanted everyone to think he was an upstanding person, the blinking Christmas tree attached to a long extension cord laying in the front yard embarrassed him. The same night, I woke up to go to the bathroom. I put on a long, thick bathrobe, and when I came back to our bedroom, he was standing in the middle of the room asking me where I'd been. He then grabbed me by the throat, put me up against the wall and said, "I will hurt you!" He accused me of being in the room with his brother, but never confronted or asked his brother. That was the very first and last time a man has ever put his hands on me! Ladies, please know that when a man tells you he will hurt you, believe him! Do not take it lightly. This man was ready to hurt me for something he imagined. If he really thought I was with his brother, why didn't he go to his brother, who was in the next room? This is when I realized that there was something mentally, emotionally, and spiritually wrong with him. After that incident, my husband said that whatever happens in this house stays in this house. I told him that if he ever put his hands on me again, I would tell anyone and everyone that would listen, including the mailman, ice cream man, and the dog catcher!

He kept the television on all the time regardless if he was home. It always stayed on pornographic channels, playing all day and all night long. Sex with him was not good; it was painful. I say sex because it was not lovemaking; it was aggressive, degrading, and just downright humiliating.

I never told my mother what was going on, but she knew, and she called my brothers. My older brother, who was a military man, came to town. He came to our house and his words to my husband were, "If I ever hear of you putting your hands on my sister, I will be back. I will take you out, fly back home, sit on my porch, and nobody will ever know what happened to you." Because my husband now knew that I had brothers (backup) who would deal with him, he calmed down a bit.

Before my brother left town, he gave me the best advice ever. He said, "The moment you feel uncomfortable in this house, get out!"

To get out of the house, you had to use a key to unlock the door. I got to where I was so frightened, I would sleep with the key in my hand under my pillow.

The Repentance Stage

There were so many things that happened during the short time we were married, and none of them were good. The next day, we were arguing, and I honestly don't remember the details. However, during that argument, I fell to my knees, and I just started screaming and crying, saying, "God, I'm sorry! I'm sorry. I am so sorry." Then the most terrifying thing happened. My husband picked me up from my knees, looked me in my eyes and he said in a soft, calm, but firm voice, "He don't hear you! I'm your God! You can see me. You can feel me. I'm your God." A chill went through my body. It was frightening because I knew it was Satan speaking to me directly through him. That's when I knew it was time to get out!

It's amazing because sometimes we don't realize the danger that we're in. But the Word of God tells us that the angel of the Lord encamps round about those that fear Him and delivers us from the hands of Satan. For me to be delivered from what was about to happen to me, the spirit of the Lord came upon me, put me on my knees, and made me cry out in repentance for my disobedience. That was the mercy of God that saved me that day!

I thank God for my angels and the Holy Spirit within me that put me on my knees and said I had to repent now! I was not in control of falling to my knees and crying out to God in front of this man; it was the Holy Spirit crying out for me. God had warned me several times in different ways not to marry him, but I didn't listen. God's grace and mercy kept me through this situation. After I had suffered for a while, God delivered me and let me know I was still His beloved daughter. Even though I didn't listen, even though I messed up, even though I sinned, Christ let me know that He still loved me and had me covered. He reminded me I still belonged to Him and that nothing would separate me from His love.

Breakthrough Stage 5

That morning, when my husband went to work, I immediately went to my mom's house and said, "Ma, I have to get out of that house!" She said, "Let's do it," as though she was already waiting and prepared. It's amazing how fast we cleared the house. I got everything that belonged to me out of that house within an hour. I just started throwing everything over the fence to my mom's yard, and as quickly as I was throwing things over the fence, she was putting them in her house. Thank God for Mama! The only thing I left in the house was the set of silver candlesticks his father gave as a wedding present. When he came home that evening, he was surely shocked to walk into the house and see that it was totally empty except for the candlesticks, his clothes, and whatever he had before I moved in.

He called me on the phone and said, "Wow! You took everything. You could have left some of the wedding gifts because they were given to both of us." I reminded him the gifts came from my family and my mom's friends, and if they knew how he had mistreated me, they would come and get the gifts themselves. He was even upset I took the shower curtain. It belonged to me and wasn't the same one he had when I moved in. My husband was only concerned about the belongings, not the fact that I had moved out.

Divorce

What got his attention was when I advised him I would file for divorce. He didn't want a divorce; he wanted us to just separate. I didn't even have to think about that. I immediately said no. I refused to be married to a man who didn't love me and treated me the way he did. I was not going to be tied down and committed to a man who was wasting my time and keeping me from having the true love I deserved. Especially while he was having affairs with other women. I would no longer be physically or emotionally abused by him.

I then realized that my husband's real concern was the house. The house was still in my name only. He wanted me to deed the house to him. I told him I would only do that if he gave me back the money I put down on the house, plus some extra for doing him this favor. He refused to do that; he said he wasn't paying me anything. I thought that was a fair deal for someone whose credit was bad and unable to get a house himself. He paid monthly rent to a wealthy stranger but refused to pay me what was rightly mine. This let me know that his true intention was only to use me to obtain the house. I told him that because he was so selfish, he would never have anything. His response was, "That remains to be seen." (Years later, I saw that my words were true.)

I found a divorce attorney. He asked if there were children or assets involved. I told him we had no children, but we had a house. The attorney asked me whose name was the house in. I advised him it was in my name. The attorney then asked me if I purchased the house before we were married, and I said yes. The attorney said my husband had no rights to the home whatsoever. A few weeks later, the divorce papers were delivered to the house. I remember I looked out from my mom's window and saw the driver drive up and give him the papers. Afterwards, I heard a lot of noise and banging. I heard hammers, chain saws, and drills. It sounded like major construction was going on next door. I said to my mom, "He's destroying the house!"

I called the police and met them outside when they arrived. They asked if there were any weapons in the house. I told them there was a rifle. The officers went to the door and then into the house and advised my husband to stop destroying the property. The officers let me know he had a right to be there because it was our marital home. They could not make him leave but instructed me to not stay there.

My husband received a citation that night for animal abuse only, for failing to get medical attention for his dog that was visibly sick and in pain. For that, he was required by the state to work with animals for a while.

When I went to pick up my divorce decree from my attorney, he informed me that my husband came to see him regarding the house. My attorney advised him that since I purchased the house prior to the marriage, in the state of Florida, he did not have any claim to it. Again, my husband was only concerned about what he thought he could get.

Enticed Back and Delivered Again

Once the divorce was final, my ex-husband had moved into an apartment, and one day left flowers for me on my parked car. This was the first time he had ever given me any type of gift. He called and invited me so sweetly to come over, saying he just wanted to see me again. I honestly cannot explain why I even entertained his conversation, but I did. A small part of me missed him and felt sorry for him, so there I went. Once there, things started out nicely, but then quickly escalated into horror. He wanted to have sex with me, and I refused. He forced me into his bedroom, threw me on his bed, and got on top of me. This time, I was screaming at the top of my lungs, hoping someone would hear. There was a sliding glass door in his bedroom that led directly to a swimming pool. I was not a very good swimmer, and I had an overwhelming feeling that he was going to throw me in.

As I continued fighting him off, the Holy Spirt was letting me know what he was planning. As I continued screaming, the spirit of the Lord let me know that his next step was to put a pillow over my face to keep me quiet. As he reached for the pillow, I felt I had no more strength to continue fighting him off. Then the Holy Spirit rose up and spoke clearly and boldly through me, and said, "You don't have the right to do this to me!" Immediately, he stopped, got off me, and said, "Get out!" I quickly ran out the door. Those were not my words, but the voice of God that spoke through me to that evil spirit. We must remember, the enemy can only do what God allows him to do. As I left, I placed the flowers that he gave me on top of his truck. After that night, I felt free again. He later called and said that because of me, his neighbors called the police because they heard screaming coming from his apartment. Two days later, my mom and I were driving, and we saw him and his former girlfriend together riding in his truck.

The next time I saw my ex-husband was years later when he had fallen on extremely hard times. It was God that allowed me to see his fate. When I saw his fate, all I thought about was the day my mom cried to him, saying she wanted to know that before she leaves this world I had someone who would take care of me. My mom was the sweetest woman of God, who poured out her heart with tears to this man who showed no empathy towards her. We, as God's children, don't have to take revenge or wish badly for our enemies; God will always avenge His people.

Thanking God for Deliverance

Lord Jesus, I thank you! You delivered me. I was happy again; my mom was happy, and life was good. I wanted to do something special for her and myself, so I booked a cruise to the Bahamas for the two of us. It was wonderful; it was my mom's first time on a cruise ship, and she loved it. Once in the Bahamas, we stayed at a beautiful resort and just had a wonderful time together. The resort was all-inclusive. We spent hours just lying on the beach watching the magnificent clear blue waves, shopping, sightseeing, attending live shows, and eating so many delicious foods. This trip brought calmness to my spirit, and I know it did for my mom as well. I was with my mom, my best friend. I don't remember ever being as happy as I was on that trip.

Upon returning home, I rented the house out for a while, which was a major headache for me. I decided I wanted nothing to do with it. I let it go into foreclosure, which I later regretted. I should have sold it.

One afternoon while having dinner at a local restaurant with my mom and one of her friends, I was sharing with my mom's friend about my marriage, what I went through, and how God delivered me. A young woman sitting at the next table got up, came to our table and said, "I was listening to your story and I want you to know I just finished writing a book about the things you just said." The young lady told me I was going to hell because I divorced my husband. I did not know this lady, but I knew of her. I knew she was recently married to a minister. Mom, my mom's friend, and I sat quietly, allowing the young lady to finish expressing herself. Then I politely said to her, "Sweetie, just keep on living." Although other thoughts came to my mind to say—one being the nerve of you coming to my table, interrupting our conversation and telling me I'm going to hell—I held my peace.

She then walked back to her table. I don't know if she understood what I meant by just keep on living. But I know life brings about different experiences, trials, and tribulations, and who are we to judge another man's sins? The Bible says we have all sinned and come short of the glory of God. I won't allow anyone else's opinion to dictate my life when it comes to Christ. After everything God brought me through, I know He didn't bring me through hell to send me there! It's so important to read and understand the Word of God for yourself. Talk to God for yourself and develop that close personal relationship with Him. Tell Him what you're thinking and feeling, because he knows, anyway. I know God forgave my sins, and as long as I know that, another man's opinion doesn't matter.

A few months later, my mom's friend advised me that the lady was now divorced from her new husband. The next time I saw this young lady was at a church event, and when she looked up and saw me, I could see the shame on her face. I don't know why her marriage ended in divorce, but I'm sure when she saw me, she remembered my words to her: just keep on living. Surely, she knows what that means now.

God's Choice for Me

Life was good. My mom and I began singing together at various quartet events around town. She met a woman who asked her to join her and her sister to form a group. My mom asked me if I was interested because she would only join if I did. We joined the group. Our group didn't have our own musicians, but that didn't stop us from singing. Each time someone asked us to perform, there were musicians ready to play for us.

Our group got along well. We met lots of wonderful people as we traveled to different singing engagements. There was one group who didn't sing much in the Miami area; they mostly performed in Ft. Lauderdale. I really enjoyed their performances! This group performed at a small storefront church in Miami that we frequented regularly. They were like no other local quartet group in our area. They were a professional, very well-dressed group of men who could *sang*.

There was one man in the group who really stood out to me. He didn't seem to stand out to others because he was more in the background as a vocalist or sometimes he played the drums. He had a serious, confident look about himself; he looked like a leader. He seemed serious about God and what he was singing. By his spirit and demeanor, I could tell he loved the Lord. He was also very handsome, and, oh my God, he always dressed nicely. He looked blessed. He kept to himself, never hanging out with many people. By his mannerisms, I could tell he was not a womanizer. I remember being at programs and noticing him watching me from the corner of his eye. I would just smile to myself. Whenever he was watching me and could not turn his head before our eyes met, he would nod his head as if to say hello. But he never actually spoke. Other times, he would wink his eye. Although I didn't respond,

I was very flattered. I was so attracted to this man; he carried himself in such a respectable manner. I heard no one speak negatively about him nor did I ever see him joking around with others during the church events. That really attracted me.

Frequently, he would talk to my mom but wouldn't say anything to me, even though I was standing or sitting right beside her. I was sure he was truly infatuated with me. One time, my mom and I were in a restaurant when he came in. He saw us and sat at our table. He never looked directly at me or said anything to me but talked directly to my mom. This seemed strange, but I took it as a compliment. He really liked me, and I liked him as well. I respect that he took his time approaching me directly. I believed he felt uneasy approaching me because I gave no sign that I was interested in him. I know it was something different about me; it was God that had a hedge around me. Not only this man, but other men within the quartet groups around town tried to get to know me through my mom. My mom is friendly and will talk to anyone. I have a more reserved personality, which I believe makes me unapproachable to some. I was not one to play games or to be taken for granted, and this could be seen in my mannerisms. My mom could see that he liked me. She told me where he worked, which was very close to our house. She would see him leaving work around 4:00 p.m. as she drove by on her way home.

I decided to let him see me in another environment other than church and away from other people. It was time for him to get off work. I took my dog with me and drove down the road. I ended up directly beside him at a traffic light. I pretended I didn't see him and drove a couple of blocks down the road ahead of him and turned into a bank parking lot. I was hoping he would follow me. As I got out of my car and walked up to the ATM, he pulled up. Wow, he talked that day! He introduced himself as Terry Morris. It was a short conversation, but I remember him asking if I liked Chinese food, and I said not really. His expression looked a little discouraged. Terry asked if I like going to the movies. I said yes. He asked if I would like to go to the movies sometime and I said sure. I gave him my number and told him to call me. When I got in my car and was out of his sight, I screamed at the top of my lungs with joy and excitement! I'm sure my dog was wondering what was wrong with me.

The next day, he called, and we had a brief conversation. We made plans for him to pick me up to go to the movies. When he arrived at my house, he came to the door like a perfect gentleman and spoke to my mom. We proceeded to his car, and he opened the door and closed it behind me. Terry didn't talk too much on the way to the theater. Once we were seated in the theater, and the movie began, I could tell he was nervous and uncomfortable because he kept twitching and moving as though he was restless. I gently put my hand in his, and like a miracle, he immediately calmed down. I saw the tension leave his body, and he became so relaxed. He did not let go of my hand for the remainder of the evening, even as he drove me home. From that day on, everywhere we went, we always held hands. It was as though our hands were magnets, and whenever we were close, they clamped together. I truly believe my hand was his calming point.

We spent every possible moment together. He would go home after work, shower, and then come directly to see me. One evening, as Terry and I were saying good night, I said I love you, and it came out so naturally; it was definitely how I felt. He didn't say it back, and I was not expecting him to, but I could tell he was surprised but also full of joy. A few days later, Terry told me he loved me and not a day ever went by that he didn't continue to tell and show me his love. Sometimes when he said he loved me, I would not say it back; instead, I would say thank you. He asked why do I sometimes say thank you, and I said because I feel so honored to have a man like you love me. He thought that was beautiful.

Terry was so helpful not only to me, but to anyone and everything that was important to me. Terry was a protector; he was willing and ready to fight all my battles, and everyone who knew him was aware of that. If I was upset about something someone said or did to me, he would approach them. His love and kindness to my mom came naturally because of the great relationship he had with his mom, who had passed away years prior. My mother thought of Terry as one of her own sons.

If I said she needed something or I wanted to buy or do something for her, he took it upon himself to make sure it was done.

Once, my mom went out of town, and when she returned, we had purchased her a washer and dryer so she wouldn't have to continue going to the laundry mat. She was so excited, she washed everything in her house, even things that were not dirty. My mom called him Baby Terry. She said, "Baby Terry, do you want me to wash your suits?" Terry laughed and said, "No B! I'll take them to the cleaners." B was Terry's name for my mother. When my mother turned sixty-five, I planned a surprise party for her. I even wrote a song for her titled "Mother, We Love You." Terry, I, and my brothers that were present sung it to her at her party and it was beautiful! Later, Terry and I recorded the song but changed the title to "Jesus, We Love You." Terry did not hesitate to pay for the entire event because to him, that was his mom who he loved and respected and wanted her to have everything she so rightfully deserved.

When Terry and I first met, I was saving money to buy a townhouse. One day after work, he asked what I had planned, and I told him I was going to look at a townhouse that was for sale. He came with me. The townhouse was really nice. It was several years old, but in a nice neighborhood. We did a walk-through of the townhouse and noticed that it needed some work done. Every time I mentioned something that would need work, Terry would say, "That's not a problem. I can fix that." On the way home, I told him I really liked the house, and asked him was he going to help me pay for it. We had only been seeing each other for a couple of months. His response was, "You must gon marry me." I replied, "You must gon ask."

After the inspection of the property, I decided it would be too much work for the price. So, I didn't buy it. One day, out of the blue, my mother said, "You know Terry is going to ask you to marry him." I responded, "You think so," and thought no more about it.

December 2001, Terry went to his hometown in Adel, Georgia, and invited me to join him later when my vacation began. Upon my arrival, Terry met me at the Greyhound bus station with excitement in his eyes. As we were stopped at a traffic light, I noticed he seemed a little distracted by what I was saying about my bus ride. He then turned to me and asked, "Will you marry me?" *Oh my God!* I was shocked, but I immediately replied, "Yes!" The traffic light changed to green, and I could see relief on his face. It was not a romantic proposal, but it was sweet. I loved it because it was from his heart. I was so in love with him and I knew he was in love with me!

I knew Terry was God's choice for me because I truly loved him, and God gave me a peace in my spirit about him. Everything just felt right. Even my mom believed Terry was the one for me.

Life/Financial Planning Begins

After we returned to Miami, we began preparing for our wedding, the reception, the honeymoon, and buying a house. Terry was the fleet manager at a roofing company where he made an upper middle-class salary. God is good because he only had a high school diploma, whereas some individuals with college degrees didn't make as much as he did.

I asked Terry what he spends his money on, and his response was mostly clothes and jewelry. This was true because he dressed to impress, and boy, did he look good! I did not make nearly his salary, but I was good at organizing finances. Terry was excellent at handling the finances on his job, but because of sadness from the death of his mom and a prior failed relationship, he was not thinking about the future. So, he did not have any money saved. But he had excellent credit, just as I did.

It's a wonderful thing when a man knows his limitations and will accept help and advice from the woman he loves. We were each other's helper. Terry was always receptive to my thoughts and ideas about our finances. He was smart and great in math, yet Terry never told me we should follow his plan or state what we were going to do. I shared what I thought was best, and he was receptive. Once Terry and I began making plans for a life together, I realized he was an excellent financial planner all around; he just needed motivation from someone he loved and who loved him. He needed a goal and someone to appreciate him and how he was able and willing to take care of them. And thank God, that person was me!

Ladies, the Word of God says in Genesis 2:18, "And the Lord God said, It is not good that the man should be alone; I will make him an help meet for him." Ladies and gentlemen, God gave Adam his own personal woman as a help meet. Notice the words *help meet for him*. Ladies, God did not create us to be *every* man's help meet. Men, *every* woman was not created to be your help meet. You must know the one who is for you! God did not make two women from Adam. He made one—the right one!

I was Terry's safe place. He could be himself with me. I listened to him; I knew about the people he interacted with daily, and he made sure they knew about me. He protected me in every way a man should protect those he loves. And may God grant mercy to those who would even think of bringing harm or coming against me. He was proud to introduce me to his friends, family, and coworkers. Just as I listened with interest to him, he did the same with me. He knew the people that were close to me. He showed love and respect for each one of them. And everyone that was special to me loved Terry as well. I loved this man because he didn't take a back seat to anyone. God created this man to walk tall, confident, and to be a fearless leader. But oh, so gentle, kind, and loving with me!

A few weeks before our wedding, I asked Terry, "Why have you never asked me if I can cook?" He said it didn't matter to him because his mom taught him to cook a long time ago. So whether or not I could cook was not an issue. Wow! Ladies, how many men would respond like that? He was not a dictator to me, nor was I to him. We just seemed to always be on the same page.

I had always dreamed of living in a two-story home. Because the townhouse needed so many repairs, I decided I wanted to live in a newly-built home. I asked Terry what area of Miami he wanted to live in, and he left it up to me. I began searching and came across a new community in Homestead, Florida. We went to the sales office, picked the home that we wanted built, and they gave us a certain time to bring in the down payment. After leaving the sales office, I told Terry that we could do this, but we would have to make some major spending changes. He was all for it. Because the house had not begun being built, this gave us more time to come up with the down payment. I already had most of it since I was going to buy the townhouse. Our biggest issue was the closing costs, but we still had plenty of time to save for that.

I asked him to bring me all his bills and his pay stubs, and I made an Excel spreadsheet for him, and I did the same for myself. I placed our income at the top and listed all our expenses for the month. The remainder of the money we would place in a joint savings account. After monthly expenses were paid and money placed in savings, we both had very little left for personal spending. But that was okay because we were determined to go into this marriage with no debt. This worked well for us! One thing the lending officer told us was that we could not charge anything on our credit cards until after the closing of the property.

Because of that, Terry gave me a wedding band set he had asked his oldest brother to place on his Sears charge card. I know many women might have been unhappy with that, but I wasn't. I knew we were on a mission. We had goals to meet, and he did what we could afford at the time. Also, I was not a materialistic woman. My goal was to be happy with the man I loved. Although the wedding set had a tiny diamond, to me it was gorgeous and as big as the world!

Terry later paid his brother for the ring. As the years passed, without me ever asking or showing any sign that I wanted another ring with a larger diamond, Terry upgraded my rings three times. The final one had a beautiful seven carat diamond. My God, it was breathtaking. God is so good! First Timothy 6:6 says, "But godliness with contentment is great gain."

Our Churches

11

One Sunday, Terry invited me to the church he was attending. The church was a medium-sized Baptist church where Terry was the drummer. As I sat in the congregation, I became extremely sleepy, struggling to stay awake. I thought of the story in Acts 20:7-12, where the apostle Paul was preaching in the upper room, and a man named Eutychus fell asleep and fell out the window. It was time for me to get up and leave because I had never struggled to stay awake in church. I knew that was not where I was supposed to be, so I got up and left. Terry later asked why. I told him what happened and that I could not attend that church. Later, that same church was involved in a scandal. Thank God for His guidance!

During this time, I had joined a non-denominational church in North Miami. I contacted my pastor and told him I was getting married, and that my fiancé and I would like to meet with him. He scheduled a meeting for Terry and me to meet with him and his wife to begin premarital counseling. My pastor and Terry immediately formed a bond. Terry joined my church because he knew my pastor was a real man of God. Terry saw the fruits of the spirit manifested through him. Terry respected that the pastor was older and knowledgeable in the Word of God, and that the pastor showed great respect towards him as well. Therefore, Terry was willing to share his gifts and talents with this ministry.

Some questions my pastor asked pertained to our relationship with the Lord, how long we had been seeing each other, our love for one another, our past marital status, if we had or planned to have children, and our upbringing. Before my pastor went further to talk with us, he said, "Brother Terry, I have one last question for you. Are you willing to die for her? "Yes," Terry responded. My pastor stated the importance of this question. The Bible says husbands are to love their wives as Christ loved the church. Christ gave His life for the church.

During our sessions, my pastor talked to us about the roles of the husband and wife in a Christian marriage—the union, sanctity of the marriage, and putting each other first after Christ. I remember my pastor saying that our marriage would be a great example to many. After our first counseling session, my pastor's wife told me something that I always remembered. I received it as a great compliment because she was an amazing woman of God. She simply said, "You remind me of myself." For the duration of our sessions, Terry and my pastor did most of the talking while his wife and I listened. My pastor's wife had a quiet spirit, but was not timid. She allowed her husband to lead, but he respected the God that was in her and that spoke through her. She was a discerning, wise woman of God. She was his backup. Like myself, she also had a serious countenance. These were some traits she could see in me as well.

Second Wedding Preparations Begin

Terry had a godmother whom he loved very much. She stood in place as his mom. Terry said she wanted to plan our wedding. Although I was not happy with the idea because I wanted my mom and myself to plan it, I went along with allowing her to make the plans.

As time went on, I became more and more frustrated with the ideas that his godmother had, as well as the attitude she projected. Terry and I were paying for the wedding, reception, honeymoon, and closing on a brand-new home. We did not want to go into our marriage with wedding debt. However, anything I suggested or told her I wanted, she would say was a terrible idea. Terry's godmother wanted the entire church decorated with fresh flowers and have real doves flying in the sanctuary. (My thought was who's going to clean up after those doves.) She did not like my wedding dress, the bridal party dresses, or the singer I chose. She wanted a certain type of glassware, and she wanted to have a certain kind of food catered. She didn't like anything I wanted for *my* wedding!

Her ideas were great if that's what you wanted for your wedding and your budget could afford it. Her heart was in the right place, but her heart and our budget were not in agreement.

After several meetings with her, one evening Terry and I were driving after leaving her home, and I could no longer hold back the tears of frustration. I started crying and Terry pulled over to the side of the road and asked me what was wrong. I told him that everything I wanted for our wedding is not what his godmother wants, and she insulted all my ideas. I had no say-so. I also wanted my mother to be involved in planning our wedding. Immediately, Terry called his godmother and thanked her for wanting to plan our wedding, and told her we decided to plan it ourselves.

Terry's actions let me know that I came first before anyone else in his life other than Christ. If I wasn't happy, Terry was going to fix whatever the problem was. This man was my defender. He did not allow me to worry or stress over anything. Terry was a real man that took his responsibilities seriously. It's as if God taught him how to love and take care of me. Everything just came so naturally to him.

Once my mom stepped in, everything just fell into place. My pastor described the wedding as royal. He also said this was the first wedding he had performed that started on time.

This time, I was so excited about my wedding day! I wore a magnificently designed white gown with a beautiful veil made by my mom. Terry looked so handsome in his white tuxedo. My wedding party colors were lilac and white, which was perfect for a July wedding. The wedding took place at our home church, which was already beautifully decorated. It just so happened that there were two huge floral bouquets that aligned the altar. They fitted perfectly with our color scheme, so we did not have to do any additional decorating. I created an elegant, romantic procession for the wedding party. As each bridesmaid approached the altar, she was greeted by one groomsman, who bowed before her and presented her with flowers. We included as many family members as possible. Most were from out of town. There were twenty-seven people in our wedding party; it was amazing. One of my admired local quartet singers sung my requested opening song. During the ceremony, Terry serenaded me with a song he wrote just for me, which he later recorded and titled "Promise to Love You." Everyone teared up listening to him sing to me. A huge reception followed our ceremony at an elegant reception hall in North Miami. It was truly a festive celebration that included live singers along with our quartet band rendering the music, while our waiters served deliciously prepared food to over two hundred guests.

We planned our honeymoon together, which was a seven-day cruise that left the following morning. Because we were leaving for our honeymoon the following day, Terry had reserved a gorgeous hotel suite at one of Miami's finest resorts directly on the beach! Words can't express how tranquil the entire atmosphere was. We sat in our private jacuzzi that overlooked the cool blue waters. We had our own personal butler that attended to our every need, bringing us scrumptious fruits and drinks. After all the excitement of the day and getting settled in the suite, we were so tired and just fell asleep in each other's arms. But we definitely made up for it the next day! Our honeymoon cruise together was amazing! We had the best time together. We were husband and wife, but also best friends.

After coming back from our honeymoon in the Bahamas, we moved into our new home. Neither Terry nor I had much. I had my clothes and a few items I purchased for the house. Terry had his clothes, a small TV, and lots of gospel CDs, DVDs, and albums. Because I was living with my mom, I did not want to take any furniture from her house; I wanted to leave her home fully furnished. Terry was living in an efficiency with older furniture. Our goal was to purchase all new furniture for our new home. We were determined to start out fresh together, and we did.

Before going to sleep the first night in our new home, I kneeled to pray. Terry kneeled beside me and held my hand. After I finished praying, he prayed. This happened every night of our marriage.

Terry was truly a leader and protector. He covered me and our home in prayer. I remember times when I was not feeling great and I would ask Terry to pray for me. Without hesitation, he would lay his hand on my forehead, and he would simply say, "In the name of Jesus!" There was no long drawn-out prayer; he kept it simple, and amazingly, I always immediately felt better.

Terry came from a large family and would always call out each of his brothers' names before the Lord in prayer. He loved his brothers but knew they had not given their lives to Christ. He always prayed for them to receive salvation. He wanted so much for his brothers to show love and get along together. Terry believed in the power of prayer, and God used him in so many ways to be a blessing to others.

Terry was always content; he was happy just being at home, although he was always willing and ready to accommodate whatever I wanted to do.

13
Our Marriage Agreement

Right after we were married, Terry and I were having a conversation about how good God is and how thankful we were that God put us together. I told Terry that to stay faithful to each other, we needed to keep other men and women out of our marriage. Doing so would keep the enemy from destroying what God put together.

I wanted Terry to keep the following in mind:

- If I can't hear it, it does not need to be said.
- If I can't see it, it doesn't need to be seen.
- If I can't go, you don't need to be there.

Terry agreed with this because it went both ways. I followed this as well. It did not mean we had to be with each other all the time or be in every conversation. But it meant that if you said something to another person who would later make you ashamed or would destroy our marriage, you should not say it, do it, or entertain it.

If you looked at someone or something in a lustful manner, which would hurt or make the other feel uncomfortable, you should not be looking at it, him, or her.

If you went somewhere and you know your presence would hurt or cause shame to your spouse, you should not be there.

The Bible tells us to put our trust in God. So, I put my trust in the God that my husband and I served. I knew that our Lord and Savior Jesus Christ would intervene in any situation that would arise to try to destroy the union that He had put together. All I had to do was watch and pray and God would do the rest. I'm not saying that temptation would not arise or that we wouldn't fall short of God's plan, but that whatever situation arose, the Lord would not allow it to destroy our union.

14

Our New Home

Here we were with this immaculate two-story home with nothing in it but love! To stay out of debt, our motto was "if we can't afford to pay cash, we can't afford it." For the first week, we slept on the floor. It was okay because it was a new home, and it was carpeted. The first thing we purchased and had installed were some beautiful custom-made wood blinds for all the windows. We were so excited about this wonderful home that God had blessed us with, and we showed God our appreciation by taking care of it and each other. After a week, we purchased a mattress, then, room by room, we furnished the entire house by paying cash for everything. Not long after we married, I was laid off from my job. I was a bit worried, but Terry said, "Don't worry, I got this. This is God's house. All He asks is that I pay the mortgage." He made it sound so simple. He told me I didn't have to work because he made enough to support us. So, for about a year, I did not look for a job. Terry handled all the bills. We would go grocery shopping and were never concerned if we had enough money. We always had more than enough. I never had to ask Terry for money. Each day before he left for work, he would leave money for me. This was not money to put towards the home or pay bills; it was just for me to do and buy what I wanted for myself. Terry always had money, and he made sure I did as well. He believed in giving his tithes and offering. That's why we were blessed and never went without. Terry was very good at handling our finances, bills, and savings.

Ministering in Song Together

Because there were disagreements within the quartet singing group, Terry left the group. I could see he missed singing, so one day I asked why don't he start his own group? I told him that Ma and I will sing with him until he get some more guys to back him up. I believed he had too much talent not to be using it. Terry liked the idea. We began rehearsing and soon added another family member to the group and a full band. As time went by, I asked Terry had he looked for some men to sing background for him. He said he was happy singing with me and my mom. Our group was called The Chosen Vessels of Homestead, Florida.

Terry had a love for quartet music and was an anointed singer—not just gifted, but anointed by God. He never took any vocal lessons. When he sang or spoke to a congregation, you would feel the power of God coming through him. Whatever song came out of him was unique, sweet, and calming. Although he had a love for quartet, he could sing all genres of music better than the original version. Terry was my biggest fan and supporter besides my mom. Whenever someone asked me if I could sing, I always replied, "I can carry a tune." That never sat well with Terry. He said, "Stop saying that; you can sing."

In the quartet circle, there seemed to be a lot of competition amongst groups. To encourage us, Terry would always say it didn't matter what group we sang after because when it's our turn, I'm bringing the thunder! And he did. He came full force with the power of God, which was the thunder behind him! Terry was a group all by himself, but he wanted his family with him. Terry was truly saved and lived a life constantly witnessing to others about Christ. It was difficult for Terry to just start singing, he always had to witness to the congregation before he sang. He would always say, "I can't just sing. I have to tell the people about the Lord." As our group and band grew in members, we traveled a lot. Terry and I went on vacations often as well. When the company he worked for had out-of-town meetings, he always wanted me to travel with him, and I loved it. Often, he would tell my mother to pack her bags and we would drop her off at her sister's, who lived thirteen hours away. Not only did he not want me to be alone, but he didn't want my mom to be alone, either.

This was Terry's first marriage, so it was amazing how he knew exactly how to treat the woman in his life. Before we would sing at programs, he would let the audience know I was his queen. He would address the men in the audience by saying you can look at her once, but don't look twice. And he meant that. He would testify how he was out on disability for a while, and I told my job that I needed to take a leave of absence to take care of him. He was so proud of me, and he let the world know it. Tery was so patient, loving, and caring. I could do no wrong in his eyes. He was a man's man. There was no fear in him. He spoke his mind when others were afraid to.

God blessed us to live in perfect peace together. We never argued and never slept in separate rooms. You rarely saw one of us without the other. This man was my husband, friend, protector, and prayer partner. He was my covering. We still held hands everywhere we went, and he continued being a gentleman, opening car doors and pulling out my chair. God prepared this man just for me because God knew what I needed in my life. Terry was the man God chose to fulfill those needs.

....

My mom became sick and passed away in July 2013. It was a day I'll never forget. It was the saddest moment quietly walking out of the hospital hand in hand with Terry and my Aunt Pat, knowing that my mom would never walk out of there again. The pain of having to leave her there is something I cannot explain. Thank God for my husband! I leaned on him for comfort and support. He was there to hold me at night while I cried myself to sleep, assuring me that everything would be okay.

16
Traumatic Ending to My Perfect Marriage

The most traumatic day of my life was in December 2017, when God suddenly called Terry home after sixteen years of marriage. My world shattered. I watched as my husband closed his eyes and went home to be with the Lord. I can't explain that feeling. My heart was broken! Someone once told me that the more you love someone, the more you'll hurt. I found this only to be true in Terry's death. Now I had no one to hold me and get me through his loss, as he was there to get me through the loss of my mother.

Terry's death drew me closer to Christ. I was saved, but I spent little one-on-one time with God, praying, studying the Bible, or even witnessing to others. I was sheltered and covered in prayer by my mom and Terry. I was enjoying the benefits of God, but not giving Him the time and praise He deserved. I no longer had the two most important people in my life. But I knew I had the One that had given me those two people, so I had to lean solely on Him. I had to get to know the man who was really looking out for me all this time.

I was so distraught that I constantly cried out to God to help me. I began having panic and anxiety attacks and spent many days being rushed to the emergency room. I could not understand why it took me years to stop having panic and anxiety attacks when it seemed that others who lost their spouse were coping so much better and faster. Terry's death placed me where I had to place all my trust in God. The enemy was trying to destroy me! I was now in a desperate fight for my life, my joy, and my peace. The enemy wanted to take all of that away from me. John 10:10 tells us that, "The thief cometh not, but for to steal, and to kill, and to destroy: I am come that they might have life, and that they might have it more abundantly." I know my God dispatched His angels because a battle had begun.

Doctors prescribed medications, but I refused to take medication for emotional pain, loneliness, and hurt when I knew where it originated from. I truly believed God could and would heal my broken heart. Psalm 147:3 says, "He healeth the broken in heart, and bindeth up their wounds." I'm not against anyone taking medication for their mental and emotional health. Do what helps you cope with the struggles of life, but it was not for me. I refused to allow the love that my husband and I shared and the faith that I had in God to lead me down that path.

Although it was extremely difficult, I put my trust and faith in Jesus Christ and His Word. It was difficult because doctors and therapists were telling me I would need medications and therapy for the rest of my life. Those words angered me. They also suggested different breathing techniques and yoga, which were not helping. Hurt is so difficult when you lose the one person who has taken care of and loved you unconditionally; the person who allowed you to be you, loved you more than he loved himself, and never criticized or got angry with you.

My husband, lover, best friend, and the man God prepared just for me was now gone. But my God said He would not put on me more than I could bear. I would read this scripture, but I struggled to believe it because I was going through so much, feeling physical and emotional pains I had never felt. I never questioned God why He allowed my husband to be taken away, but I blamed myself.

The only thing positive I could see from Terry's death was that it drew me closer to Christ. I thought if I would have spent more time with Christ, seeking and doing His will for me, that Terry would not have died. I believed God was punishing me for not putting Him first. I carried that guilt for a while. Then I realized Terry had completed what God had for him to do and would not punish Terry for what I did not do. Terry loved me with all his heart, and he showed it every day. He loved the Lord with all his heart and was always busy with kingdom work. Our pastor performed the eulogy and said he had never seen so many adult men cry at another man's funeral. Terry was a role model for so many. He also said that Terry was the best deacon he ever had and wished he had ten thousand more just like him. Terry was truly a man after God's own heart!

17

Dream of Victory

I felt like I was losing the battle to regain my joy, peace, and physical strength. I was praying, fasting, and using all the faith I could muster. But every time I felt better, suddenly I would feel worse, and I could not understand what I was doing wrong. I know grief is different for everyone, but after six years, I was still battling the same physical and emotional issues. Then God gave me a dream that I held on to.

In the dream, I was driving a school bus up a steep hill. Seated on the passenger side was my mother, and in the rear behind me was my brother. I was very afraid, so I told my mother that we must get off the bus. My mother said, "No! Stay on the bus!" Suddenly, my mom and brother were gone from the bus and I was all alone. When I looked ahead of me, I saw the enemy in human form looking down at me, waiting with excitement for me to fall backwards. This entity saw me struggling but seemed to have gotten joy out of not helping me. Then the seat I was in seemed to turn into a swivel chair which swiveled me up right beside the enemy. He would not look at me but kept looking straight ahead. I punched him in the face with no remorse and watched as tears rolled down his cheeks.

God interpreted that dream for me. I knew it meant that I was not to lose faith concerning my emotional healing. It also showed me it was an evil spirit that was fighting against me, waiting and watching for me to fall. But in the end, the enemy would be the one in tears. My friend, Minister Kathy Fullenwider, told me that my mom and brother, who were on the bus, were actually the Holy Spirit, which had been with me all the time. The Holy Spirit was telling me not to lose faith and to hang in there. Even though I could not see Him working things out for me and often felt alone, He was and is always still present with me.

Hebrews 13:5 says, "For he hath said, I will never leave thee, nor forsake thee." Christ reminded me I have strength through Him to overcome every obstacle in my life. And He let me know that Satan, who was trying to destroy my mental and emotional health, would be defeated, and I would come out victorious.

18 Restored

I can truly say this ordeal humbled me. I was never one to ask for help; I had to cry out to strangers walking by for help, or God would send them to me. I remember on one occasion feeling fine, then suddenly, I was sitting on the pavement of the parking lot of my job shaking. I could not walk and could barely talk. My heart was racing, I was crying, panicking, and didn't know what was wrong. I had my phone in my hand, but did not have enough strength to dial 911. I cried out to a stranger walking by, asking him to call 911, and I remember him saying that my phone was in my hand. I told him I tried to dial but couldn't. He called 911 for me and stayed with me until the paramedics arrived and took me to the hospital where the doctors diagnosed me with having a panic attack.

On another occasion, I experienced the same scary symptoms, but I managed to drive myself to the emergency room; however, I could not walk to the entrance. I was getting ready to call 911 to come and get me from the emergency room parking lot when a woman walked by and saw me standing by my car. She asked if I needed help. I said, "Yes. Will you please help me get inside the emergency room?" She put her arms around me, bracing me, and helped me inside the emergency room. Later, she came back to check on me. Again, it was another panic attack. I lost three great jobs after my husband passed away because of my emotional state.

One neighbor that had just recently moved into the home next to mine invited me to come and stay at her home. She did not know what I was going through. She was a blessing because we had only seen and spoke with each other in passing for a short time. She lived alone but traveled a lot for her job, so she wasn't home very much. She gave me the entry code to her house and told me to make myself at home. I stayed there for a couple of weeks. I later thanked her and asked her why did she welcome me into her home when she really didn't know me? She then said something that has always stuck with me. She said, "I didn't know you, but I knew your spirit!" And that went both ways—her spirit agreed with the spirit of God within me.

When Terry passed, I knew I could not continue to live in our home because the memories were too much for me, so I put our home up for sale. My plan was to move to another city once the house sold. In the meantime, I needed somewhere to stay. Terry took his last breath in our home, and it was extremely difficult for me to be there with that memory. There was a woman who attended the same church as me who I had never had a conversation with. But the Lord placed it in my spirit to ask her if I could stay with her for a while. Her home was closer to my job. She said yes, welcomed me, gave me a key and the alarm code to her home with access to come and go. I asked why she felt so comfortable welcoming me into her home when she really didn't know me. I received the same response as that of my neighbor. She said, "I didn't know you, but I knew your spirit."

Although I felt alone without Terry, I now know that God was with me every step of the way. He knocked down all the strongholds that were against me and put the right people in place at the right time to help me.

I am now a witness that my God heals a broken heart! He allowed me to smile again. Jesus Christ restored me! He healed me! He delivered me, and I certainly came out victorious. Christ placed prayer warriors in my life. He even put strangers in my life that came to my rescue. I know Terry is smiling. He was probably one angel God had fighting for me!

I give God all the praise for everything He has done in my life. We all have a testimony. Ladies, although my marriage ended suddenly and sadly, please do not let that discourage you from accepting true love. I wouldn't trade the times Terry and I had together for anything. Of course, I wish it would have been longer, but I'm so thankful for the time, love, growth, and learning God allowed us to have together.

Conclusion

I know the angels rejoiced over my marriage because God truly ordained it. If you meet someone and there is any doubt about who their God is, you need to reconsider your relationship with that person.

One couple's experience is not everyone's experience. I can only speak regarding my marriage. God put Terry and me together. He knew exactly what each of us needed in a spouse. Our relationship flowed so easily. There was no such thing as making it work; it just did. We didn't need time away from each other; we wanted and enjoyed being with one another. We never dictated to each other what needed to be done. We automatically knew and worked together to get it done. There was never any yelling, putting one another down, or sarcastic remarks. I don't claim to be an expert in marriage, divorce, or the scriptures, but I serve a God who is! I know that if the relationship makes you feel uncomfortable in any way, and you cannot be who God created you to be, that's not the one for you. If you cannot be yourself or feel you're always walking on eggshells around them, reevaluate the relationship. If you're not loved and returning genuine love, do not stay. If you're living in fear and not being respected, protected, and covered, this is not who God has for you. Remember, Jesus forgives our sins!

Jesus loves you. Wait on His choice for you!

About the Author

Wandala Morris was born in Gaffney, South Carolina, but spent most of her life in Miami, Florida. In her spare time, Wandala enjoys spending time with friends and family, watching movies, and writing plays. She loves traveling and meeting new people. Wandala loves the Lord and devotes herself to working within the church ministries. She dedicates herself to encouraging others about the importance of a personal relationship with Christ, drawing on her life experiences. Her successful marriage allows her to share valued lessons with others for a thriving, healthy marriage. Wandala is passionate about letting others know that despite their faults, sins, or shortcomings, Christ still loves them, and if Christ is pleased, another man's opinion doesn't matter.

www.ingramcontent.com/pod-product-compliance
Lightning Source LLC
LaVergne TN
LVHW052004060526
838201LV00059B/3837